Easy Learning

Handwriting Workbook 1

Age 5-7

Karina Law

This book belongs to

How to use this book

- Easy Learning workbooks help your child improve basic skills, build confidence and develop a love of learning.

- Find a quiet, comfortable place to work, away from distractions.

- Get into a routine of completing one or two workbook pages with your child every day.

- Ask your child to circle the star that matches how many activities they have completed every two pages:

Some = half of the activities

Most = more than half

All = all the activities

- The progress certificate at the back of this book will help you and your child keep track of how many ⭐ have been circled.

- Encourage your child to work through all of the activities eventually, and praise them for completing the progress certificate.

- Each workbook builds on the previous one in the series. Help your child complete this one to ensure they have covered what they need to know before starting the next workbook.

- Help your child to rest their pencil in the 'V' between their thumb and index finger; their fingers should be between one and two centimetres away from the pencil tip.

- Introduce your child to the 'starting point' in each activity, where they should first place their pencil or pen on the paper.

- You may find that it helps your child to say aloud the patterns and words as they write.

Parent tip
Look out for tips on how to help your child with handwriting practice.

- Ask your child to find and colour the little monkeys that are hidden throughout this book.

- This will help engage them with the pages of the book and get them interested in the activities.

(Don't count this one.)

Published by Collins
An imprint of HarperCollinsPublishers
77–85 Fulham Palace Road
Hammersmith
London
W6 8JB

Browse the complete Collins catalogue at
www.collins.co.uk

First published in 2011
© HarperCollinsPublishers 2011

10 9 8 7 6

ISBN-13 978-0-00-727756-8

British Library Cataloguing in Publication Data
A catalogue record for this publication is available from the British Library

Written by Karina Law
Based on content by Sue Peet
Design and layout by Linda Miles, Lodestone Publishing
Illustrated by Graham Smith, Andy Tudor and Jenny Tulip
Cover design by Linda Miles
Cover illustration by Jenny Tulip and Kathy Baxendale
Packaged and project managed by White-Thomson Publishing Ltd
Printed and bound by Martins the Printers, Berwick Upon Tweed

MIX
Paper from responsible sources
FSC
www.fsc.org   FSC™ C007454

Contents

i is for insect

Patterns: Spider bungee jump

1 Draw over the broken lines to make four spider threads. Start at the green dot.

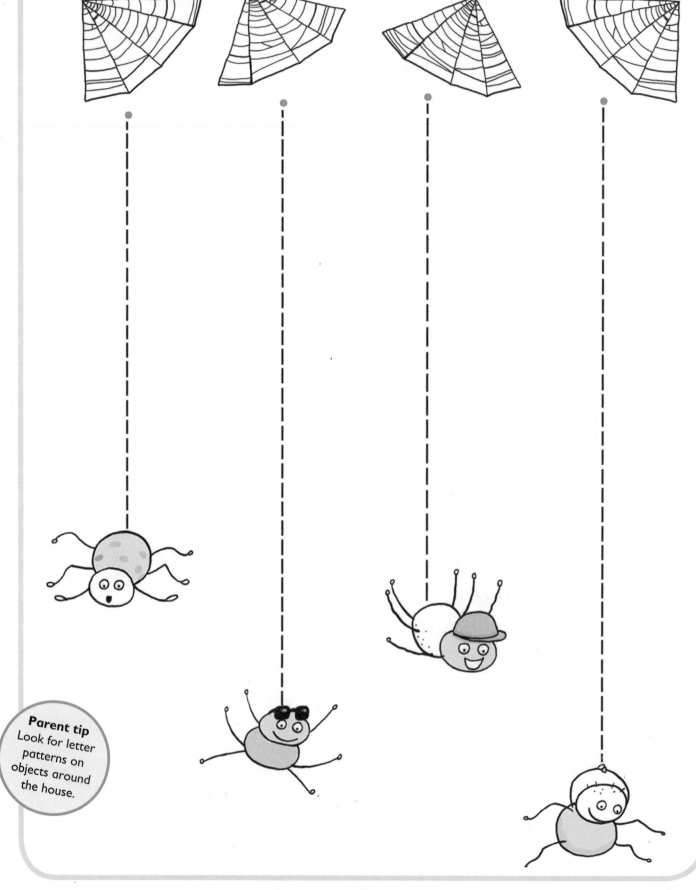

Parent tip
Look for letter patterns on objects around the house.

Patterns: Jump for it!

Trace over the broken lines to help the frog hop across the river past the hungry crocodiles. Start at the green dot.

How much did you do? Activities 1–2

Circle the star to show what you have done.

Some

Most

All

Patterns: Bouncing beach balls

1 Draw over the broken lines to show how the four balls bounce. Start at the green dot.

Parent tip
Call out the patterns your child makes when writing words – for example, up, down, round.

Patterns: Letter shapes

2 Draw over the broken lines to complete the patterns. Start at the green dot.

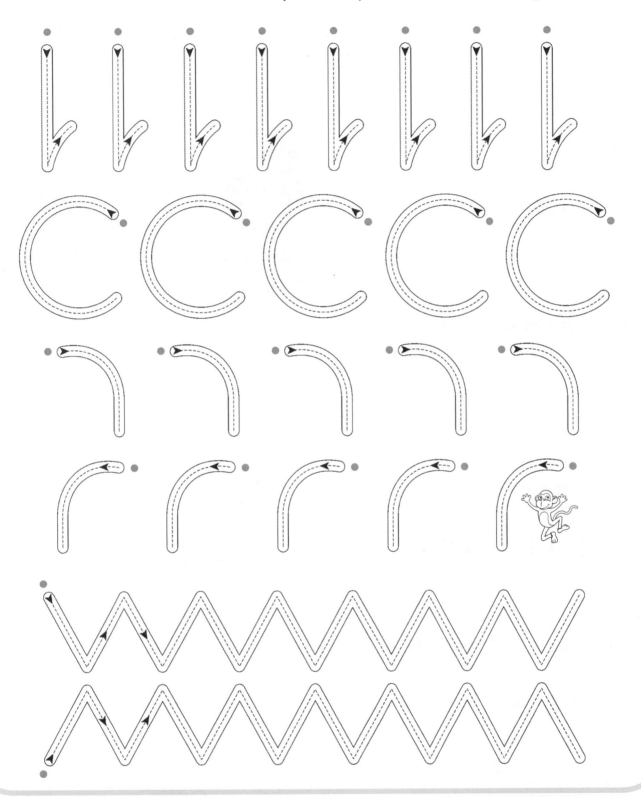

Letter shapes: l, i, t

1 Trace and write. Start at the green dot.

l l l

Trace the grey letter l.

l is for lion

2 Trace and write. Start at the green dot.

i i i

Trace the grey letter i.

i is for insect

3 Trace and write. Start at the green dot.

t t t

Trace the grey letter t.

t is for tiger

4 Practise writing l in this sentence.

All lions like to lunch.

5 Practise writing i in this sentence.

Tiger Tim is feeling ill.

6 Draw round the teddy, beginning at the green dot. Write t on his tummy.

How much did you do?   Activities 1–6

Circle the star to show what you have done.

Some   Most   All

Letter shapes: u, j, y

1 Trace and write. Start at the green dot.

u u u

Trace the grey letter u.

u is for umbrella

2 Trace and write. Start at the green dot.

j j j

Trace the grey letter j.

j is for jam jar

3 Trace and write. Start at the green dot.

y y y

Trace the grey letter y.

y is for yo-yo

Parent tip
Get your child to practise writing letter shapes in wet sand or with finger paints.

10

4 Practise writing u in this sentence.

Huddle under an umbrella.

5 Practise writing j in this sentence.

We enjoy jogging.

6 Practise writing y in this sentence.

A yawning yak.

Letter shapes: r, n, h, b

---

1 Trace and write. Start at the green dot.

r   r   r   r   ·   ·   ·   ·   ·   ·

Trace the grey letter r.

r is for ruler

---

2 Trace and write. Start at the green dot.

n   n   n   ·   ·   ·   ·   ·   ·

Trace the grey letter n.

n is for nose

---

3 Trace and write. Start at the green dot.

h   h   h   ·   ·   ·   ·   ·   ·

Trace the grey letter h.

h is for house

4 Trace and write. Start at the green dot.

Trace the grey letter b.

b is for bear

5 Practise writing r, n, h and b in this sentence.

Nine brown hens running backwards.

How much did you do?   **Activities 1–5**

Circle the star
to show what
you have done.

Some   Most   All

13

Letter shapes: m, k, p

1 Trace and write. Start at the green dot.

m m m · · · · · ·

Trace the grey letter m.

m is for mouse

Parent tip
Watch closely to make sure your child follows the direction of the arrows.

2 Trace and write. Start at the green dot.

k k k · · · · ·

Trace the grey letter k.

k is for koala

3 Trace and write. Start at the green dot.

p p p · · · · ·

Trace the grey letter p.

p is for pencil

4 Practise writing m in this sentence.

A monkey jumping on a trampoline.

5 Practise writing k and p in this sentence.

A pair of kangaroos hopping on pogo sticks.

Letter shapes: c, a, o, d

1 Trace and write. Start at the green dot.

c c c · · · · · ·

Trace the grey letter c.

c is for clock

2 Trace and write. Start at the green dot.

a a a · · · · ·

Trace the grey letter a.

a is for apple

Parent tip
Remember to ask your child to find and colour the monkey.

3 Trace and write. Start at the green dot.

o o o · · · · ·

Trace the grey letter o.

o is for octopus

4 Trace and write. Start at the green dot.

d d d

Trace the grey letter d.

d is for deep sea diver

5 Practise writing c in this sentence.

Five scared mice caught by a crafty cat.

6 Practise writing d in this sentence.

A duo of daintily dancing dinosaurs.

How much did you do?   ## Activities 1–6

Circle the star
to show what
you have done.

   Some

Most

All

Letter shapes: e, g, q, f, s

---

1 Trace and write. Start at the green dot.

e e e · · · · ·

Trace the grey letter e.

e is for *elephant*

---

2 Trace and write. Start at the green dot.

g g g · · · · ·

Trace the grey letter g.

g is for *goat*

---

3 Trace and write. Start at the green dot.

q q q · · · · ·

Trace the grey letter q.

q is for *queen*

Parent tip
Practise joining the letter combination qu with your child to help with spelling.

4 Trace and write. Start at the green dot.

f f f · · · · · · ·

Trace the grey letter f.

f is for fairy

5 Trace and write. Start at the green dot.

s s s · · · · · · ·

Trace the grey letter s.

s is for strawberry

6 Practise writing f in this sentence.

A frog hops after a fly.

How much did you do?   Activities 1–6

Circle the star to show what you have done.

 Some   Most   All

Letter shapes: v, w, x, z

1 Trace and write. Start at the green dot.

V V V

Trace the grey letter v.

v is for vase

Parent tip
Look at different fonts and letter styles on a computer with your child.

2 Trace and write. Start at the green dot.

W W W

Trace the grey letter w.

w is for whale

3 Trace and write. Start at the green dot.

X X X

Trace the grey letter x.

x is for x-ray

4 Trace and write. Start at the green dot.

Trace the grey letter z.

z is for zebra

5 Practise writing x in this sentence.

Six foxes in boxes.

6 Practise writing z in this sentence.

Snoozing zebras.

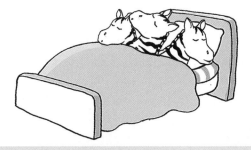

Letter joins: short vowel a

1 Trace and write.

 bat   bat

 rat   rat

 cap   cap

 tap   tap

 bag   bag

 van   van

Cat on a mat.

Cat on a mat

22

Letter joins: short vowel e

Trace and write.

 pen pen

 hen hen

 ten ten

 legs legs

 bed bed

 web web

Little red hen.

Little red hen

How much did you do?   Activities 1–2

Circle the star
to show what
you have done.

Some

Most

All

Letter joins: short vowel i

1 Trace and write.

 zip zip

 ship ship

 bin bin

 pin pin

 fish fish

 dish dish

Jack and Jill went up the hill.

Jack and Jill went up the hill.

Letter joins: short vowel o

Trace and write.

dog dog

log log

cot cot

mop mop

shop shop

sock sock

Fox on a box.

Fox on a box.

Letter joins: short vowel u

1 Trace and write.

 sun sun

 bun bun

 jug jug

 mug mug

 bug bug

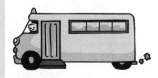 bus bus

A duck in a cup.
A duck in a cup

26

Letter joins: sh, ch, th

2 Trace and write.

sh   sh   sh

ch   ch   ch

th   th   th

 shoe   shoe

 sheep   sheep

 chips   chips

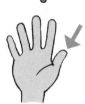 chair   chair

thumb   thumb

3 three   three

How much did you do?   Activities 1–2

Circle the star
to show what
you have done.

 Some   Most   All

27

Capital letters

1 Capital letters don't join to any other letter.
Trace and write. Start at the green dot.

Capital letters: parcel sort

2 Choose different friends to give each gift to. Write their names on the labels. Remember to use a capital letter at the start of each name.

Big wheels

1 Trace over the broken lines to draw a tractor and a bus.

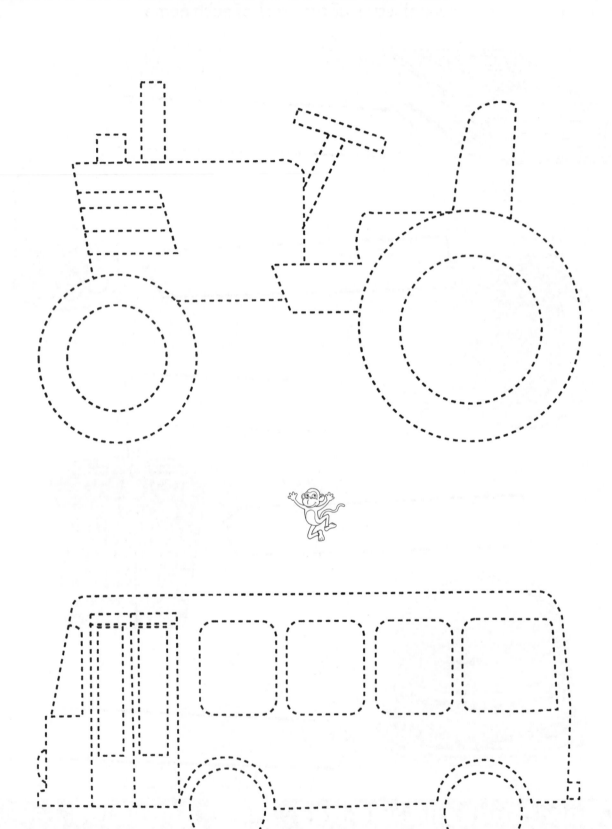

Handwriting practice: 'Ip dip dip'

1 Write this poem in your best handwriting.

Ip dip dip

My blue ship,

Sailing on the water

Like a cup and saucer.

How much did you do?   Activities 1–2

Circle the star
to show what
you have done.

 Some   Most   All

Check your progress

Did you find and colour all **15 monkeys?**

(Including this one!)

- Shade in the stars on the progress certificate to show how much you did. Shade one star for every ⭐ you circled in this book.
- If you have shaded fewer than 10 stars go back to the pages where you circled Some ⭐ or Most ⭐ and try those pages again.
- If you have shaded 10 or more stars you are ready to move on to the next workbook. Well done!

Collins Easy Learning Handwriting Age 5–7 Workbook 1

Progress certificate

to

name _____

date _____

Patterns		Letter shapes: l, i, t, u, j, y		Letter shapes: r, n, h, b, m, k, p		Letter shapes: c, a, o, d, e, g, q, f, s		Letter shapes: v, w, x, z	Letter joins: a, e	Letter joins: i, o, u, sh, ch, th		Capital letters	Big wheels Hand-writing practice
pages 4–5	pages 6–7	pages 8–9	pages 10–11	pages 12–13	pages 14–15	pages 16–17	pages 18–19	pages 20–21	pages 22–23	pages 24–25	pages 26–27	pages 28–29	pages 30–31
☆ 1	☆ 2	☆ 3	☆ 4	☆ 5	☆ 6	☆ 7	☆ 8	☆ 9	☆ 10	☆ 11	☆ 12	☆ 13	☆ 14